Longitudes & Latitudes

Longitudes & Latitudes

Phoebe Angeni

gatekeeper press™
Tampa, Florida

Longitudes & Latitudes

Published by Gatekeeper Press
2167 Stringtown Rd, Suite 109
Columbus, OH 43123-2989
www.GatekeeperPress.com

The editorial work for this book is entirely the product of the author. Gatekeeper Press did not participate in and is not responsible for any aspect of this element.

Library of Congress Control Number: 2022947890

ISBN (paperback): 9781662933639
eISBN: 9781662933646

to the shoulders on which I stand
to those who talk to their flowers

thank you Mum and Goose

Course: Heading, Bearing

Venus: Dawn by Garnet

love poems for all kinds.

Love you, honest

If you've never received a love poem, this one's for you

I love you like a garden rake
in the fall because you clean up nicely and are a bit of a trip hazard

like a folded up umbrella,
which speaks of sunshine and safety from storms

I love you like we're uranium glass teacups
teetering on a fragile caffeine high

as an insect fossilised in amber
curiously, timelessly, heartstoppingly

I love you how glitter spreads –
a little too much and in all the wrong places

like a manual fluid extractor:
in a useful, kind of gross and sexy way? I don't know much about cars.

I love you loyal, true, in *Midsummer*
as Helena says: 'I am your spaniel,' but with self respect –

dragon's-egg-close,
that is to say hoarded precious, dangerously

I love you like candles, wind chimes, and the letter q
because they're unrelated:

pea shoots climbing chicken wire,
rising hexagonally, harmonious, entwined

I would love you even if you were a dung beetle, honest.
Ok maybe less then, but I'll love you. Promise.

Aurora

what if we *both* got on our tiptoes to kiss
dancing up into the clouds – higher
except the clouds were cotton candy
and stuck to the bottom of our bare feet,
taking turns to twirl each other marigold
arm under arm under the pink and blue sky,
which you'll remember is cotton candy –
only it sings like sparrows when you touch it
and we're tiptoeing, so it's like a symphony
of birds that are turning into harps,
flying on strings attached to something
behind the candy, whirling like gears
a yarrow sun – only the gears grew that way like roots
from the ground up, arm under arm over tiptoes
melting into the gears, the strings, the birds
the touch of rustling silk air,
falling through it all, which is also cornflowers
blowing us higher, slightly swimmy, slightly sticky
remember – cotton candy sky

Saturday

the morning cracks –
spilling embryonic
decadent, molten

diffused in bed
as butter on toast with egg shells
broken awe – jaw and sky

watch the incense fish unfurl
into a liquid breeze,
swimming around eddies, heady to scent

our chamomile smiles and smoky whispers,
shimmering sweet
as the desert haze before hallucinations

Gorgeous

to the cheekiest café on Bell St
xx

first light turns her key in the catching lock
flips the lights, boilers set to purring,
berries on the counter, a surgeon's floured arms –
it's Greg James o'clock in the morning

Tones and I, swaying my hips,
trays of tit-size scones in hand, swinging
ding! order in
SMASH: an entire cutlery drawer to the floor

pigtails bobbing – not like that
with *laughter* as the regular shift rolls
their eyes, to the monitor upstairs
to find some shred of patience

to the bustling window
where mummy's little treats have flown
off the shelves
'I bet those two are on a date'

'*I* bet we need to refill the jam jars
and *don't* lick the spoon,'
which I wasn't going to do anyway
because I snuck some earlier on toast

8:49am

rippling blackbirds washed the sky
over the rumbling potato truck –
alongside the cobblestones
the street crawls to coffee shops

a sprawling collection:
sprinting briefcases in hand, heels in another
stragglers with faces of one night stands
and me, clutched tight

love-crumpled inside a paper bag,
baked just this morning – a resurrection
over-filled with berries,
spread generously with cream

Phoebe Angeni

the lie-in

there's a time in the morning
(about 9am in February)
when the whole world is bathed
in that post-sex glow –
you know the one I'm talking about:
when everything slows down,
light cuts across the grass
golden – through the wings
of little insects, rising
and falling along the treeline –
everything alive, buzzing
(although the air itself is still)
the world is quiet – breathing
breakfast for the birds
and for me in the kitchen –
spider threads across my window
glittering

May

let's lay on our backs in the hammock –
see if we can talk to the gods
through our eyelashes where the sun peeks

if there is fire in the rubble
there is something left to burn
if we reach up the willow tree might just catch our fingers

often I feel like a dandelion weed
I've said it before,
sprouting up unwanted through sidewalk cracks

baked earth, anywhere I can rest my legs
rooted between souls that have been sucked out
and replaced with khaki

I blow myself into wishes – gods silent as the Royal we
a spider dangles off my fingertip, spinning
as constellations somewhere I can't see

Phoebe Angeni

Sisterland, Yosemite

in summertime we wear Flowers called Susan,
and Mud, and beaded rites of passage –
all tangled up in memories
like campfires, primary
education in shade-loving and Dogwood Trees.

we sit under Mountains in summertime.
They move, Mountains – very slowly
and gave me granite veins and a craggy heart
to stand in Rivers with schools of fish –
i move like Merced, and the fish move like me.

When we were Four

Best-friend-ships sail on cold-bum days,
and warm-bum days, one-way
tickets made like towel rooms for changing –
hoisted high to laughing spaces, winking in the dark.

Unparalleled records in border transactions –
it's all easy music and dreams coming true.
Honey forever, honey honey, puzzle adventures
full of pivotal moments and shameless cajolery –

Honey, best-friend-ships sail on certain tides,
on tables and times called Constant – Understood.
Make your one-way ticket like a towel room – together
and sparkling, just high enough to reach.

Getaway drivers, group hugs, hot mamas –
we're on similar wavelengths, and we come in many flavours
stronger than morning breath.
And honey, forever, these puzzle adventures
I don't like – I love. Endlessly.

Argos

how can I recall the love of a limb, a vital organ
my own heart, beating –
an old man now,
but only in the second pair of legs

salty as the bay, which you constantly smell of
splashing through the surf – a toothy grin
dappled through the afternoon –
light and willow trees

when we were young the bathtub was the sea
and I taught you to swim
so now you love it with me, grinning
for the time we spend together

like sailboats depend on the breeze
on the horizon
your head pressed into my hands
a prayer – the entire world

Butterflies

Lost is a kind of mist – carried suddenly
A change in shape. A change of direction.

Dandelion seeds make zeroing in harder, while
Butterflies fly erratically so they're tough to catch

I am also tough to catch. Romantically.

Danger flaunts its colour in lower pitches
And I become the sizzling edge of a fire,

But my secret weapon is under my wings,
Bright like the sun and smell of lemons.

Hooked

when I glanced at you, we laughed
into a catastrophic storm

and I was tight-roped, dissolving
towards a synthetic shimmering sun –

sudden cravings for carnival lights
roared lion-like, leaping through hoops

for sweets to brush themselves against my lips
without a beckoning

I was popcorn, hopping
drenched in butter, dash of salt

applause invades my ears –
and the crazy thing is I don't care

towards the beacon, teetering
between the edge of ecstasy and nowhere

Third Degree

Noon is a brazen goddess
unabashed, unashamed at the sun's peak
she rushes to the apples of your cheeks
smothering your face in kisses

she'll eat you alive and you'll love it –
the freckles marking you as hers
where she bathed your forehead, shoulders, nose
with adoration to blistering

she's a kind of goddess we need
to be loved so close to burning
to swelter in desire and fan our necks,
melting strawberries in the pitcher of Pimm's

she is the truth and tells it plain
no condolences – she points out
the cellulite on your bum and thighs
and to her, it just *is*

lit from all angles – the way she likes
reddening under her eye

little death

flickering candlelight makes less of form
tracing each corridor – divinity
settles heavy in the air, sweet

goddess in repose, undone
in elegance –
emboldened eyes dare, serpentine

across breath – each liminal
and catching
space

at the altar – obsidian smile
mischievous as the setting sun
glitters wicked, whispering psalms

House Party

flies come for the water
and I come for the flies –
to see their nausea, juxtaposed
against the treacle flowers in her cheeks –
to see her dazzling red-framed bones.

if I had to admit, I like the sound
how I like wrinkles and raw meat: well seasoned
well spiked – boozy like a backhand slap
reverberating in the cloister – that laugh,
which sends them all buzzing.

like I said, I come for the flies
for the poison-curled smiles squished to their lips,
for that something of primordial ooze –
sprouting sour, delicious crush
and drip-drop-dripping down.

Phoebe Angeni

Pairings of Light
6 haiku

Phaeton
flickering light reigns
the horse-drawn hand of the sun –
spring bulbs turning on

Moon
we meet in the glass,
smiling at our reflections
framed by the window

a caterpillar
discovering it's future
noses the cocoon

Autumn Leaves
wildfire growing
slow by the rushes
of the slumbering pond

Lovers
a dreich afternoon –
puffing through the rain
twin chimneys

18

Promise

it's just you and me on the page
meeting here – sometime, someplace
maybe sitting outside, wrapped up at the beach
you could be on a treadmill, in a passenger seat
in bed with me late at night, writing this
somehow, somewhere in motion –

my voice is an echo of your eyes
sharing the narrative – a dance of minds
you know, I kind of like that actually – us, this
shape-shifting around in between syntax –
touch your little finger to the line
just here –

do you feel that? electricity?
just kidding, but it's probably nice paper
nice to stop, to breathe
I'm on the other side of the sheet
I promise you
beneath the ink

Topsy-Turvy

have you noticed we're head over heels
in the water drops – the condensation
running down the mirror in the bathroom?

well, we would be if we could focus on one drop –
eyes blur – we merge into shades of brown and beige on blue (or grey)
something else inside the fogged up glass

leans against the towel rail – casual.
my dentist says I brush one side of my teeth more than the other –
I said I guess I just lose focus,

toothpaste dribbling off my chin – see? lost focus.
spit. rinse.
without a towel again – see?

don't peek while I get one,
or better yet look at the water drops – the condensation.
pick one and you'll see: I'll be upside down running – pink and beige on grey.

made of something like the stars

falling through each sky – the monolith,
rising ring ding lights, and buckle-up clicks –
airships crash through cloudlike creatures
ripped through the howling wind, wicked
up by the sea, sunk low
black as asphalt, glittering as fishes

we play with fire, molten, magnificent
slumbering magma burning slow –
glowing flames like sunflushed cheeks –
the smoke's our favourite and it knows,
woven into living tapestries
by lovely fingers burnt with love

hold me together again

is it bad I like the way bruises colour my skin?
drinking in the purple-blue like twilight,
the fading sickly yellow days
just something interesting, you know?
that says you've done something, been somewhere
been affected by some part of life, like a scar I guess
like you've *lived*
exactly: bruises are temporary – fleeting
I don't even know how I got this one.
you know monarchs migrate to Mexico?
they fly such a long way –
just a thought, you know, fleeting
hold me closer, put me together again

Here and Now: Cumulus by Oak

existing somewhere between page and divine.

Waking Up Early

as night drains from the sky
and daylight swirls in its wake
the sisters go to wash their hair –
scenting the air,

nebulous hounds must again rise
to begin their merry chase.
hunter follows with bow,
eyelids flutter slowly

opening to light.
a clatter of dishes –
warm scents greet me,
no Pleiades to meet me.

Company at Breakfast

out of death emerges life –
a cosmic rearrangement
of silence, blossoming
[   ] and life and death
a cosmic rearrangement
jolting from and into silence:
the sacred morning

startled life and blossoming:
Time's wings were
[   ] as
death-catching sunrises
yours and mine
with outstretched hands
for certain passage

Phoebe Angeni

Thoughts I had while making toast

a fairy ring of fly agaric springs
somewhere in the forest
from a central point
where the mycelium fell

expanding – a woodland supernova
a tiny Big Bang
to the cosmos –
a grand watchful eye

stirring between blades of grass
winding nowhere and everyone at once
darting between breaths, atoms, space
is creation

is life in absence.
it's a thought I think of often
romanticise even –
possibility, ideal:

the perfection of nothing
Everything to be built
Everything to be gained
liquid caterpillars in their cocoons

entropy is nature and vice versa
it's fun, sorrow, the rebellion of throwing ourselves to the wind
just to feel something, you know?
or say we felt something. Important. Rolling my eyes.

that's called finding your audience,
called to witness your moment, your being
that free tumble – ungraceful
impactful, avalanche

whether or not you want to jump out of the nest
become all new kinds of broken

Transform

Dear St. Andrews,

I wonder if in a hundred years
when I'm a hundred twenty three
we'll come home to your wind-swept streets
and all be grey together

'It's so nice to see you.
I've missed you, my friend.'

will we still go on drives and sing?
and do all of the crazy things
we wouldn't even dream
to do without each other?

'It's so nice to see you.
I've missed you, my friend.'

will we remember how we learned
to see each other's hearts
and love the worst and best parts
we whispered mostly to the ceiling?

'It's so nice to see you.
I've missed you, my friend.'

99A

sweet things seem to vanish
before they've truly arrived
like the spray of fresh clementines

we're drifting from the easy road
from new-washed hair and sleep rubbed eyes
but I'll do it, am doing it – to taste fresh clementines

I'll watch the muscles in my hands jump
over the ticking metronome
to break the spell – each trip around the sun

blinked into existence – an ant, the whole
a stop on the bus
now smelling of fresh clementines

Phoebe Angeni

Presidio

morning is the same everywhere –
darkness and the stars in fixed positions,
looking up into the night's
bright horseshoe smile.

the air is chilly just like everywhere else
in my ears – wind and the birds,
the shade of palms
against the blue.

nobody's around
my singular footsteps
and (blessedly) lonely shadow,
which is the same everywhere.

I don't know about forwards or back
or if everything's just 'for now'
the earth we are tied to, the bodies we are tied to
are stories playing out.

without the cars –
the scent of eucalyptus follows close
and Orion surveys the wooded scene
as he does
every morning.

Bright Ghazal

Truth only wakes in the darkest night
what seems good *is* good – what's beautiful's bright

she and me – rosebud mouth in the car's backseat
mummy's eyes (alone) were high beams bright

we drive forward, phoenix-like. why? we know –
Icarus falling burnt radiant bright

thousands of miles from the sea I love best
her turbulent waves vivid blue and bright

resplendent Phoebus reins the chariot –
a bundling brow etched luminous bright

pearlescent things left unsaid glaring back
on reflection – not too brilliant, nor bright

Landlocked

the wind is strong today,
so red-tails fly low, screaming.
I feel it in my leg hairs
as ants bustle along their paths,
as blooming roses sway.

silence is home to poetry
(which isn't necessarily a good thing)
nestling into breathing space –
bees into honeysuckle
bodies in mass graves.

it's all ok, I guess – or will be
if I close my eyes,
pretend the helicopters are the sea –
I miss the periwinkles, sliming along
creating sweet small lives from decay.

Bad on Purpose

my name means playful, defiant, strange
endurance. enduring. elderflower.
a derivative of my mother
torrential downpour and chocolate (to excess)
chasing light, moth-like
to the point of incineration
like fire, tangling around myself
        charmed, I'm sure,
the ghost on the stairs philosophises –
a classic, well-read with dog-eared pages
beans, bacon, and eggs at breakfast
at night – Dionysian rites in the graveyard
a by-product of my environment
cinnamon. cloves. cobblestones.
a blushing band of wave-kissed sky

Babel

I sing myself into vintage gold,
peeled back across a metal frame, a broken oath
dazzlingly overbold.

She dances sharp retorts, dry wit –
a dialect of irreverence, composed
and cracking like dogma and whips.

He adds in quick-lines, impressioniste
en plein air, poured words as silk clothes –
un portrait par coincidence égoïste

while They bask in memes:
classic references juxtaposed –
today's sun on ancient relics, newly exposing

something underneath the babble
we'll ask the silverfish – she knows
this thrumming, an echo under each tone.

our oracle scrabbles by my empty tub –
maiden, mother, sacred crone
vibrational harmony of dust and bone.

Apollo's Bitch

I live very -ingly
I do my best writing when I've just woken up
like I'm a truck driver with her arms fallen off and stuck on a pedestal
Bitch you look [pretty] damn good in the Louvre
I tell myself I lie myself I tell myself
even though I'm not supposed to ___
because I'm a Woman – monstrous as Achilles on PMS

Militant, aesthetic, and composed as fuck
fuck is a construct to show you're cool
hip with the kids
down and dirty
rites of passage
a manner of behaving
stuck on that restraint and [polite looks] like I've got [the bitch face at rest]
the way that butterflies are probably assholes,
while caterpillars shit way more than you'd expect and manage to be endearing

Nature is death and sex, but I'm sure not dead and I'm not getting any ___
I write I write like a game of operation before I speak
or you get those [big eyes like owls are turning] to people –
[I'm afraid and I love this] Artaudian bullshit.
In bed I sometimes lick my plate like a cat
and watch people dissect [salt-cured] hotdogs on screen
- an Illusion

Sent from my iPhone

New Peepers

can't stand this rosy vision
the headache of these shades
is astigmatic, idealistic
sky is B – L – U – E
BLUE

the crystals by my optic nerves
say I might go blind one day
for now I see too far ahead
blessed with 'could be' vision
and no way to make it true

over everything I *wish* I had
a blander, less-pink view
these touchable clouds are G – R – E – Y
GREY
double vision, cross eyed – here and far away

Other Names, Still Sweet

I'm called a bitch – 'cause you *have* to be
like the spice and crunch of a grape seed
pretty rough and tumble (sometimes with commas)
a harlot and a queen

rascal, rambunctious – 'cause I grew to be
like an orange rolling off a laden cart
quick with my hands, quicker on my feet
eye-catching and smart

they call me sublime – 'cause I'm moved to be
like the cross-eyed tang of a plum
myself, a wonder – all at once
to devastate and be overcome

Blood Ghazal

I grew up late into tea and a blether, but
a streak of American roams wild in my blood

I left the memories behind in a taped attic box –
seven years regenerates, down to the blood

you must remove your name to howl with the moon –
whose ties to the water run thicker than blood

cities swathe through lineage, they return as they came –
transplants: fierce nations and warring blood

you will be taught: don't depend on promises, love –
it was simpler when the Fates would write futures in blood

once the stars wink out, flushing pink, I stride:
Amazon, Angeni to the last of my blood

Eos

[from Ithaca, Edinburgh Fringe]

ancient, infinite
I danced with thunder and savage demons
who lurked in the mire
of the battlefield behind closed eyelids

there I heaved charred breaths
of ash and ember
deep into my lungs as I curled tightly
around the fading western candlelight

then I was nourished by that inky night
introspective void
where I found the stars
singing lullabies, glimmering brightly

now I am spacious
stretching languidly –
emerging golden from the rich earth
where magma transfusions rush into my veins

and I am vital –
body monumental
to my glorious imperfections
touched by sinuous rose electricity

at the dawn of time
you'll find me rising
to light the midnight blue
of the sky afire

New York

silence is a dinner
which someone else has cooked
and which you are now eating

looking out from the porch stoop
at stoplight moons, flickering like seasons,
relishing every bite

remembering last spring's pink trees
with string tied around their fingers –
when scents sang floral on your tongue

of being young and at the beach,
watching waves breach upon the shore
each and each a new beginning

The North Sea

the swooping swallows know
and the cherry blossom trees
that there are, have been, will be
many more broken and dashed than me

I like the sea – ah
she sees us and smiles serenely
hushes bluffs, skims a stone
washes worry from our bones
swirls in pools where I (alone) smile back at her serenely

the swooping swallows know
and the cherry blossom trees
that there are, have been, will be
many more broken and dashed like me

I like the sea – oh
she sees us and smiles serenely
kills a gull, heaves a sigh
crashes waves onto our thighs
nibbles at the sand and sky and smiles, serenely

the swooping swallows know
and the cherry blossom trees
that there are, have been, will be
many more broken and dashed by me

Market Street

10 minutes 'til the bus
my fingers listening
across the cobbled street
to where the flute man plays

people pass like grey hairs
cut short and curling
as the tune of smoke canaries
in a burnt orange cage

10 minutes 'til the bus
my pockets full
of me and no more troubles –
cast out to polish in the waves

PurpleAir

A phrase of cello swims the wind –
he comes to the woods to play.
it's the thing to do in *these days*, really
escape the city, the politics, the plague.
sitting on the ground – the concrete bit
right before the grass starts,
I tap bits of Fur Elise on my leg
and think about how this moment will age
like blackberries, hanging rotten on the vine
like mink, draping, drenched in red.

the foghorns make themselves known
sporadically, dispassionate
as conversation bursts through the leaves –
the rest of the audience is late, bobbing about
finding seats – they say 'the sparrows
are singing more beautifully *these days*.'
the hummingbirds and myself agree –
they're certainly nicer than the blue jay,
maybe even nicer than the cello
since everything slowed down.

Coyote Magic

it was August when we met,
panting in the summer heat
(somehow unseasonable)
a song curled in your mouth,
sleek as light-slanted leaves

our eyes glowed -yellow to green
and I waved like eucalyptus

as the birds darted, roses bloomed
a tacit understanding
like fruit dropping from heavy trees
natural as thorn-pricks
berry-stained sin

through the window where we met,
rising early with the sun
(almost unreasonable)
morning nested in my ears,
wisped by baby-haired sleep

our eyes glowed -yellow to green
and you bowed like cypress

Timeless
4 haiku

spider
snapped gossamer string
sky-diving from the ceiling –
my honoured guest

she
sweet Wisdom's dual
as a coin flipped in mid-air,
shade on sunlight-poured hair

swept skyward from the tide
sun-baking, sea-salted slurp
poor snail, happy gull

fossil
in Moroccan earth –
the shadow of a grape seed
pressed to ancient stone

Phoebe Angeni

Topography

[From Ithaca, Edinburgh Fringe]

as I come home
I barely recognise this map of rivers
colourful cairns and prayers along the pathways
the simple request for peace

something I almost remember
I think it's my eyes – like how you grow up
and catch the taste for coffee – or sprouts – or something
my eyes could get a taste for myself

coming home through little recognitions
memory and actuality – the subtle difference
scars you can't see
the marks we accept, the marks we made

gratitude is fleeting in the body
and even I have to earn my trust –
out of my wounds
I am cruellest dealer

I wonder if I know the way home
I little recognise it
I wonder if I know anything
if it's all bullshit.

(unscripted) conversations

at the crepuscular time of moths
selfhoods found and lost
to the ebb and flow of cloth

to the electric buzz of dressing room lights –
translations of the faded stars
written into dawn by night

by masks who speak for the immutable gods
through thick-painted graces
studied carefully from frauds

from the grand-swept circles to the jam-packed stalls
we're different and the same
once the final curtain falls

Wi-Fi

I live in a one-room fishbowl – every day is circle swim
memes, memes, memes & MEMEME: tinder tender

Thousands of fish does not mean plenty
b/c millions of fish means obscurity.

At 11:44 at night when I'm alone
that's something to think about.

It's just the state of things,
I'm not lonely.

Pathetic?
Quiet.

Parallel: Hammer by Looking Glass

poems that watch the world around us
and want to smash most of it.

Phoebe Angeni

Riot O'clock AM

dawn attacks are a fantasy trope,
but I can't imagine a full-fledged riot
in the early morning – only aftermath:
seven homeless, asleep on the street,
one window with a fist-sized hole (well punched)

then someone smashed the door to Walgreens
around six am.
wafting in for first brew, a man
in blue: 'Good Morning.'
I've never liked cops,

upholding-much-of-nothings,
less the law. behind the bar,
sticks out a fugitive tongue,
while above the N95
my eyes derive a new flavour of smile.

I've seen what uniforms do
not to me: white
polite: 'How are you?'
rolling your eyes: 'It's one thing after another.'
and I say I can understand

one thing after another,
but you see, I hope the glass *keeps* smashing.
it's break society or be broken – one after another
down on the asphalt, understand?
you leave with your coffee. it's Riot O'clock AM.

RSVP

it's no secret I hate Rules
can't keep false company,
you know the kind, with half-shut doors and silence
seated at tables where you don't get to speak

it's like growing up in San Francisco,
over-run with Twitter bugs, WASPish disparity
classically exclusive, down-your-nose mean
as costs up and people out onto the streets

this city used to be for real rebels
beyond bones and skin – breathing, breaking, ugly, free
put-yourself-on-the-map deviant with dirt-churned gold
now chipped and faded into forgeries

not like my wild East Scotland,
my brutal and beautiful sea
my stripped bare castles collapsing into themselves
into stubborn, resilient history

where I might live one day
she's not an illusion and doesn't pretend to be
I caught a scorpion with my bare hands before I was 5
we get on – each word I say as guarantee:

I don't belong where I was born.
some grand design or accident decreed
that I should blow across the earth – on wind
on fumes, on cherished certainty

I'll build castles of self-hewn tables
dance in mud, splattered paint, in sovereignty
stand on crumbling turrets, blowing raspberries at the world
you can come join me

Summer Black

Wearing black in the summer is physics −
cool people *will* wear black this summer. It's even biology.
          edit: 'summer black is back and not just for emos'
it's for all the contrarian views aired in summer.
How many bananas make a bunch? Push yourself farther.

Black Sea Atlantic Ocean Spiny Gear Bluefish Flounder: currently unavailable
Did you know − one of the world's most expensive ingredients is Instagram?
Its beautiful appearance is catching: Deadly America, decadent truffles,
detecting floral notes, notes of cinnamon, of bullshit.
Forget swimsuit season when there's black!
We crack open − ankles, knees, and shoulders like crabs −
that Scandinavian look: all breezy loose lines, never shapeless.
Nothing says Summer like black spiked straps on a leather biker jacket.

Headphone audio makes be-Lethe of summer black −
It's Stygian, baby − free flowing and forgetful…
Where the hell are my keys?
Sent back in time to play video games − its near-impossible to avoid the urge
and maybe the void just wants pizza − the darkest shade gets a bad reputation.
Nobody has 10 memes for every wo&man who loves to wear black −
we also have a little boat that floats on the Thames.
So many nice blends of music, honey, and charcoal eclipses in a cardboard tube.

I pierced my ear to make it mine −
only one person knows, but now you do too
          − don't read in to that.
If you split the moon you'll find a geode. Every time.
Don't read in to that.

Secret Bunker

there's a trickle of oil
then the sound stops –
skeletons in lab coats
smoking pipes, scissors
in their pockets
brown, beige, and grey
tubes in shiny metal cases

three whistles for fallout
internal memo:
organise casualties, ammo, shells
as the world cuts its teeth on postal bombs
on anti-tank missiles

those were the last words, you know?
a drug we used to take
      how strange will it get?
a couple years ago he faked his death
the same cyclone he was waiting for
last week's envelope in the mail
in the ditch

Sold the Nation

it sounds trite – the stillness
'the battle of the soul of the nation'
for the soul? something like that
which you *know* was coined to get the Christians
to shift the swing states
and the California Cynic in you rolls her eyes
rolls the wondering joint in her hand – maybe
it's not so far from the truth
like when the caterpillar you found on a plant in your garden
grew up to be this scary-looking black beetle and you feel
betrayed because all the other caterpillars just like it turned out
to be pretty moths and this is *definitely* a magpie situation, but
what do you do? do you let it out into the world even though
you know it's a tree killer because otherwise the moths will die
in captivity like the hope in Pandora's box and you'll end up a
Medean moth-killing bitch?

I think that beetle's the soul of our nation.
just me?
the joint wants to know –
when did people get so goddamned mean
so *nosey, toogoodforyou, forthis?*
so much goddamn tension in the air –
when did we have to invent the word shithole?
whoever did was a poet
like the dirt-nosed freckle-faced kid with a mop of straw hair,
representing the whole of the corn-growing Midwest, leaning
against the wall outside the town's only convenience store that
sells nudi-mags, sucking on a lollypop, breathing in dust like
second-hand smoke, watching the world go by in a 1950's
Cadillac convertible seventy years along chugging through a
2020 world and thinking:
'I can't wait for the day I get out of this shithole.'

honestly I get it, man
this nation can be a shithole
and it sold its soul to the dollar long ago

All-American: Hooked on the Orange

populous cities often see red.
dominating our perspective,
the height of coke production
sliced right through the clouds
creating a solely-scarlet sky

spring's pink sinks to delicate gold by summer,
still, at the border: a beacon of smothered salmon red,
only a few tables and for small parties only
that can be clipped / to shape /
an eye catching new form

more atmosphere means more molecules,
yet we're told the simple classic's three ingredients:
dense + sweet + tart = perfect
reliable, low maintenance, easy to clone
Repetitive Red by Behr at Home Depot

you *could* get hooked on the orange –
unstable air from the west,
smoothies fresh, free from preservatives,
the longer the path, the more removed – troubadours
of different wavelengths, scattering

Phoebe Angeni

Over 70 Different Taboo Words

Karma is a bitch –
bitchin' began in the 1950s & was found to be cool or rad
she was free, impetuous, wild, beautiful –
until she burnt out like a melted crayon – boiled, busted
as in 'life's a bitch' or 'she sure got the bitch end of *that* deal'
the Kool-Aid drinkers will tune in:

New York won't get vaccine today because Trump's a petty [censored]
a [spitefully bulk-bought 1ply bitch]
'made one's self a bitch' (Russian : ссучился, Romanised: *ssuchilsya*)
who needs evidence? if I say so it must be true!
tyranny begets violence (and vice versa)
we're all @RobertOppenheimer sons-of-bitches

sons of strong or assertive women
[WARNING] Don't try me, bitch. I'm head bitch in this house.
they bitched about the service, the ambience, the bill – *Bitch, guess what?*
a powerful, full-swing slap in the face. front of the hand.
Success, Money, Sexuality, and Power – all through intonation –
a Bitch takes shit from no one.

Quarantine Watch

neighbourhood busybodies are out
walking newly incontinent dogs –
the premise today is to borrow an egg
from my house – always *my* house.

peering in the kitchen window
at me in my underwear
just trying to pan-fry some lamb chops for lunch.

ponytailed hair over stretch pants
and auras of disdain,
looking into my windows
always *my* goddamn windows
I never look in YOUR windows

shrill white-teethed voices exclaim
'Anything new at your house?'
there's nothing new at my house.

not for you anyway
not when I'm in my fucking pants
just trying to fry
some goddamned lamb for lunch.

Phoebe Angeni

Shared Spaces
4 haiku

you kept me awake
again tonight – you're lucky
murder's illegal

good – you're not home!
now I don't have to give
your door the finger

Coffeepot
spectres through the house
none of us are awake
in the early morning

'fancy seeing you here,'
the bags under my eyes
greet me in the mirror

The News

is the pointless shutter-snap
of an antique film camera –
its unblinking, cold eye fixed
on me and you

or the polar bears – clean air
and *real* ice, not that thin stuff
crumbling into the sea

it's desert suffocation – parched
and unforgiving beige, blistering
tastelessly on the skin

or road-kill, poked at with a stick
to shake death out of decomposition
and make the feasting flies drone louder

like a foghorn's bellowing echoes
tumbling through the mist –
calling the gist of a bad situation
to owls in barren trees

San Francisco: September 9, 2020

morning smoulders, pitch black
eye-stinging, seething orange,
simmering hourly deeper
like a barbecue's char.
the plants grow hungry for photosynthesis
and I go hungry for light.
I cannot light a candle –
the smoke – my lungs – the world already scorched.
outside it looks like night – high noon
fiery orange, still searing through the fog.
the daisies hang their heads
the cedar, blackened, silhouettes
it's a quiet, sad calm.
salutations from hell, I guess.
maybe this is what the firebird saw
before the brightness left its eyes –
in a wildfire, every bird's a phoenix
and anyways, we're all combustible.
looking out – sallow, the earth – fallow
this could be the end of the world.

San Francisco: September 11, 2020

grey soot on my potted roses
and fresh air is a filtered thing.
I let the spiders move into my walls –
at least it's something, you know?

when the world is covered in a layer of death
and hungry fires rage on, eating us up
remember the towers?
killing each other, killing the world

I guess it's only fair the world kills us back a little
it's all an ego trip anyway
to think we could kill a whole planet,
like with the dinosaurs, right?

cocky shits – the Earth never died
She doesn't mind her evolution
a great big planet and *we're killing it?*
She knows better – we're killing ourselves.

Cassandra

I was bored one day, so I looked up my name – Cassandra
turns out Cassandras are very prone to hysteria,
you see, we utter true prophecies and are *never* believed,
as always, Ideology unseats Reality –
paving the road to fascism.

pessimists of the Trojan people,
every Cassandra is a blessing, liar, madwoman
taken for granted, for transcendence,
gripped with psychic possession –
the best that will ever happen to you.

we Cassandras have always been attractive with long hair,
loved to destruction, a favourite rape scene in Greek art
[enter Ajax, time suspends]
C: 'thou hast destroyed me, ~~my love of old~~!' (cut)
successful dating is ~~about really giving people a chance~~ (change)

Ghost Scissors

three Sisters spin, measure, snip
the lives of every mortal, yet artists paint three *others* Grace,
exalted. 'We cannot exist without Them,'
the Weaving Aunties told Her this since She was small.

you see, men are tricks of the mind with character –
old school swizzlers, twizzlers, and freaky-deaks,
switching from sitch to sitch, language to language,
stalking their prey with 'I think you're beautiful.'

Authority and Tradition are not easy marks –
these brothers sleep in rooms with fortified walls.
She will cut crooks in their mouths to mirror Her disfigurement
– the Glasgow smile.

She-children believe what we are told –
cultivated flowers, perfumed, grown biased by design.
this product has been cancelled. sorry!
– you do NOT have to match up both sides.

Phoebe Angeni

Strong Women

[from Ithaca, Edinburgh Fringe]

I have faith in Strong Women.
we are the poems that don't belong,
don't leave a problem un-dealt with, carrying
universes in our hearts,
happiness on our own

backs bent against imposturous winds, syndromes
of patriarchal fraudulence.
uncertain, distracted, stressed, Society drives us jealous –
mad for media validation, a mirror equal to our glow,
representation beyond object, beyond sex

we use our bodies as *we* want, assertive,
grounded between passivity and aggression,
pivoting, finding our sweet spots, rolling
otters in a creek / with the punches.
we're powerful and ask for what we want –

to be seen, respected, believed
with the weight given to gods, as
femininity is divined beyond gender
beyond chromosome – woman is a vibe
outside of language

we *are* at our core, expanding
beyond the mould – we are breakers and menders
defiant beyond barrier, gentle creatures
who hear the wail of the world and answer together
who are rallied by its cry.

Holding the Door

for the PAs

what's the password? chivalry is gender neutral!
it's the code of opening doors – everything's unlocked
*lights four-oh-five holding the door.

but young people aren't raised this way, right?
this is the NUMBER ONE assertion that salts my popcorn
*lights five-oh-eight holding the door.

I always hold doors, so I'm a hero –
those who wriggle through the gap? total assholes.
how long have I been here? a minute? a minute-and-a-half? two?

most times I'm just grouchy, but *this* gets me enraged.
[holding it in] someone take over this tacit social code!
yes – this is about you green kitten-heels, and you too eyebrows.

I try to expect nothing. a minute-and-a-half? two? a meditation
a cynic – fighting facetiousness 'til my death
*lights five-ten and go

A Beginner's Guide to Caring for your Houseplant

I like my people like I like my plants: Alive.
But there are lots of ways to kill your [potted] friends:
My plants are dead – and faux foliage isn't easily perishable.

They tell us we'll feel better having greenery about
'creating our own personal ambiance.'
Personal ambiance is what cologne and plants have in common.

Take Your Houseplant for a Walk Day only comes once a year.
That day is July 27th.
That means plant-shopping day is July 26th, okay?

Even the toughest plant is not indestructible.
They're hot, they're cold, they're dying of thirst – then *drowning*
And they never tell you. They expect you to guess!

They say you can make a plant love you if you keep things simple,
But I've diligently hydrated and still killed.
Plants are fucking fickle.

Everything is Fine

in the darkest days these words appear,
clinging to the damp sand like a chipped seashell.
Syn: It should be fair weather
worrying is natural to the mind, is nature.
when did it all start? Chernobyl, perhaps? before?

things still aren't ok since Trump is out of office –
treating a symptom doesn't cure disease.
Syn: Gonna be just fine
oppression, bloodshed, white supremacy, corruption
countless treatments, still cancerous.

he wants marriage and children / she wants to dream
beyond massacring hours, sleeplessness, contagion.
Syn: This should do the trick
even the dead are resting, having lived a full life –
inhale humanity, exhale impotence.

28,470 days that any of us will be alive:
a satire, but not exceptionally funny or good.
Syn: Gonna be ok
watching it all on my iPad at 1.5x speed to save time
classic ostrich – keep your eyes closed. everything will be fine.

Phoebe Angeni

Graduate

like a cold welcome
to a closed race – now you've less to line your pockets
to keep you warm at night

> 'the sun shines in my mind anyways
> I like to keep things simple up there –
> the same thoughts, just re-arranged differently'

things were so good in the little town
then, before, still – now they've forgotten you
the castle crumbles endlessly

> 'did I mean to paint it like that?
> I know it looked different
> but it felt like this – aye, shining'

Hired

the rain falls on my skylight
like student bills to pay
thank goodness for my heating blanket
and rainbows in the distance
fingers crossed I get a job today

I almost crushed my finger in the door this morning
like an egg
like my brain, fractured away

[inhale, exhale]

fingers crossed I get a job today

Not Allowed in the Café

for my four months in corporate coffee

there's a man has hooks for arms,
likes coffee <u>black</u> – but with sugar, cream, and straw
and sneaking behind the espresso machine
to touch syrups with his face.

a woman's scars down her nose
would *like* a drink she can't afford,
so she screams 'You're going to hell!'
blasted down by lightning – by God – by minimum wage

by some dipshit leaning in the window to shout
'YOU SUCK!'
guess he doesn't want a latte then,
not from me anyway.

once someone shuffled in her socks
wanted tea, but peed with the bathroom door wide open.
asked to leave, pleading 'where's your humanity?'
not allowed in this café.

Unmoved

Face flattened by crutches
clutched tightly
to the right and left:
stomach flesh, oozing around
the sound of train announcements.

Low brow, lower brim
of his black hat.

Dangling roots of his jeans –
wiry Greybeards –
serene,
as if fishing
under the empty dock of benches.

Low brow, lower brim
of his black hat.

Phoebe Angeni

Calisthenics to the Sun

on the bridge
beige-ancient woman
hands lifted to the sky

whether in prayer or exclamation
at the sunshine – to the sun
or in simple calisthenics

am I watching for a sign
or cardio? I get the feeling she'd know
but my bus has already gone by

The Worms

if you see a grey gentleman in the grass, it's best to leave them be.
they're distinguished and must continue on their way,
unbothered by brief rainstorms,
as any worm shepherd will tell you.

'all the soil is alive,' she reminds me.
'crumbly, cool and mild on the skin, gourmet
as breath, bones, blood, tributaries of sweat broken down
into origins of everything you see. yes, even clouds debut

under the earth, an idiosyncrasy
to consider, sun-baked, on a blue-sky day,'
she instructs, patient. this is of course about the worms
and restful ooze, which birthed and grew

architects of subterranean filigree.
'now, should these nobles wander from safeguarding decay
it's still playing god to re-direct them,'
she whispered and withdrew

beyond this plane to memory.
so, allow the gentleman on their way –
they're unbothered by brief rainstorms,
as my worm shepherd would have told you.

FlowerBomb

since I was small, I've always walked on my toes –
ballerinas don't have it easy, man! have you seen their feet?
discovering you're not average is pure luck,
comes with pain – the price of being seen

of controlling the weather, mind-bending metal,
carving the wind with your voice –
ephemeral, turned on, weird, different
words twisting through the body a hundred ways, a wound

a grand design, a slight against local authorities –
my fantasies turn to violent storms,
change landscape into armour, assembling over my body,
which was once a holding room:

before I was alive, I was living
with day-to-day darning, poking needles to my skin
to salvage pieces of construction – everyone has this in common
a little bit wild, yet it's never talked about

no one wants to feel wrath, hatred
in their home foundation, as buttress for normalcy.
I'm new to the neighbourhood, when no one's looking
I'll sow the concrete street with wildflower seeds

Evening: Dried Peony by Bone

loss. trawled up fresh from the bottom of the sea.

Phoebe Angeni

Nobody

[*From Ithaca, Edinburgh Fringe*]

if my heart cannot sing – it isn't Ithaca
that land is where I'll rest my bones

where are the sails – tie them tight
set the compass and the rudder
of my lonely boat
or let go – it does not matter

the fight has left me
and moved on for Ithaca

I'll find my love once I'm in Ithaca
once there, I'll finally rest my bones
if I must wander
I'll wander to Ithaca

we all sail alone

All my Love

Aristotle said 'the poet should speak as little as possible in (her) own person'
this is not a moral issue – this is a Cheetos issue.
I am the same person as I was two minutes ago: speaking,
buying shares of self-love conditional on appreciation,
painting failings into fantasy, because that's where my reality is:

no hot water for days, and on and off heating (currently on)
and on and off power (currently off)
fantastic
I'd tell you more but postcards are small haha
singing epically out of suffering, of sorrow, in the (cold) shower.

it's kind of fitting, I guess – falling, craving validation, getting up again,
collecting myself to myself, glued back with gold
like pottery or a pen to paper.
what *was* I thinking when I placed that last stamp?
Miss you lots, hope you're well, and in terms of letters: tag – you're it!

Left Unsaid

Chaos is an alluring way of life – impossible to leave
as small town drama or the last biscuit in a tin:
engrossing crises, chronic overwork, red flags blazing
in every relationship – Dido's pyre at Carthage
seems cosy compared to the fire-fanning stares –

ladies, I am speaking about exes: boring, abusive,
or simply and suddenly g o n e
while *we* try to evolve between each clean-up we didn't see coming –
don't you *dare* act clingy with the idealised past
because puppy-love only means they might still wee on the floor

might absorb you back into boundary-less Chaos
until you're sixty, spinning each other's madness,
repeating certain phrases, patterns of mess and lack – upheaving
until you SNAP to never hello again
until you make your bed with left unsaid.

The One that Got Away

this show's been dragged out and running long
>*Tricked to Lisbon on a plane by the dashing detective-noir*
exalted amongst your past amours
entrancing heroes of a bygone age
>*He has the gall to tip his hat, sombrely waving from the tarmac*
did someone's face pop in your head?

he's dead to us, and buried. you're caught
>*The memory plays into his mind – how good it was to kiss her*
in a wistful curse, lovingly trapped in longing
in an excellent pace, interesting plot, dynamic soundtrack
>*... sombrely waving from the tarmac*
preserved in a parallel universe.

incorrectly valued over stars and present scenes
>*In the rain, he tilts her head back, revealing matching tattoos*
pulled back to quarrel, plead, dote upon, discard memory again and again
he got away. he's gone. again and again.
>*... waving from the tarmac*
he broke your heart, after all.

Muse

I understand the illusion – cinematics
la la landing in fantasy, on swept off feet – tumbling
into the grand theatrics of it all, kept in an otherworldly box, preserved
shadow-like in chiaroscuro – the light and dark of it.
something that slips away, from me at least –
the concept, definition, understanding,
which I think sometimes to be a curse – an isolation
like the Mariana Trench, filled
with known and unknown burbles of bulgy-eyed fish
staring blankly – and bioluminescence.
that's what self is to me, today at least
'and who cares about tomorrow,'
yesterday says, moulding in unwashed dishes by the sink.

I guess I don't have much control of any of it
electricity, surging, a spotlight – divinity – something
pulls me through whether I can or want or will
and I love it – that unbridled feeling
and I fear it.
I used to wish I could pry your eyes open with toothpicks
just so you could see some glimmer, a gasp, the shape of me behind your light.
I used to hold illusion in mouth as reigns – pounding the dirt
to say love is real, constant, mouldable as clay.
it's hard to let go – not of you in particular
breathless, pouring through muscles, veins
synapses exploding into wildflowers –
first light bulbs of the industrial age.

Declarations

loving someone (to me)
seems like clutching at straws.
we seem to be clutching at straws
in opposite directions.

I do not care.
I do not brush my hair.
I crumble cookies in my kitchen
sitting on the tile floor

because you wormed your way
inside my heart
and ate it from the inside out
like wasps in a tarantula.

Bad Ritual

I carved our names into a candle
when you didn't come back –
burnt the beacon's wick black.
you shut your eyes, so it wasn't there.

I buried us in the dirt.

A frog died later on in the week

trapped between the window screen
and glass – we shared our grave,
emptiness upon emptiness given
to gods in the ground.

libations poured, roses
broken apart in my hand
into nothing.
under the earth the frog was small, patted down.

A/B Simple.

Before you love me let's keep this simple
One night. Us two.
                 – and a thousand blazing fireflies.

Before you say so let's keep it true
For now. A few.
                 – like the creases by your eyes.

Before you love me let's keep this simple
Only once. Sans encore...
                 – or three words a million ways – I ...

Don't start that sentence – Stop! Before...
Just this. No more.
                 as promises all turn to lies.

Unrequited Theme

Yesterday runs up to me (shirtless) on the beach,
jumping off the pier
at a dangerous height.

he puts his feet in fire to hear me shriek,
cuddled into my lap –
a world away
the tide pulls further out to shore.

what were your eyes trying to say? mine were saying
I love you
stay.

a suitcase
dragged
unceremoniously through the woods:
Clandestine, New York.

I'm jealous of seashells I find on the beach –
empty
and beautiful.

do you think about me tucked into
your stupid
Antarctic
bed sheets?

do I catch you?
fray you like a rope? snap
you back from reality?

I still have the picture somewhere on my phone,
fingerless gloves,
an empty audience seat.

Phoebe Angeni

Decisions

heartbreak is a song
with a plodding refrain
a snapped string
frayed rope
a bird you have to kill

a door you have to close
that shuts in your face
or isn't – wasn't – there
like turning the lights off
when it's daytime again

it sings to the tune of 'should'
wish – why – us – always
a hangnail – constantly catching
an outstretched palm –
empty

The Heart Grows Fonder

Alone's condition is knowing what it means not to be
separate, dismembered – a phantom limb
the matching glove, the one that was lost.

although she knows better and does so (sometimes)
Alone sits quiet at the end of a call
a moth – detaching life from electricity.

Alone is eclectic and likes her peace
like she likes her wine – poured out
into long silences, on the drawing room floor.

farting loudly, swearing loudly, singing
in the kitchen, bathtub, garden, street
Alone, she does what she wants, motherfucker!

Alone weighs, stinks, languishes
drowned and pale and unseeing
forsaken – bloated on a beach

(which I'm not allowed to think about).
Alone is the tundra – all these hyphens, reaching –
stark, an impression, a you-shaped space

a vacuum – void where prohibited
the concept of a minus sign – division.
Alone knows best what her name means.

Opiate

I could close my eyes to walk
around the wee auld toon –
it might be because it is so small
the streets so few
that it seems crammed – chock full, in fact –
heartbreaks of a different hue.

note the harbour there –
of fitted stones in shades of brown
Gatsby's green light – will o' the wisp
and crash – blue waves cascading down.
our footsteps (four) were red, I think
as you lead me there astray

past colourful crab traps in the drink
moored boats bobbing in the bay.
tightrope-walking on the edge,
our heads in separate spaces,
my heartbeat in my mouth that day
I would have belonged to you.

the afternoon lay on my bed
and looked up at the sky.
you counted freckles on my neck
time shrugged and passed on with a sigh.
our words were huge, the room was small
and shadows on us grew.

as your red handprints on my arms
left other places bare,
ah how I wished that red to wander –
it did. you left me there.
without the smallest backwards glance
I was hypothermic-blue.

my thoughts now are the graveyard grass
or jagged shells and broken stones –
I climb carefully over them
towards something different on my own
because of each 'last time' I saw you
this time I hope it's true.

The Crowd

bustling Styx is quiet with choked-back vows,
mistrustful hearts in Asphodelian limbo,
sole monotony.
we were all Strong Individuals – successful, self-sufficient,
drawn to unreliable, emotionally distant

crowds of Fools on arcane journeys
who stacked our decks with swords and toppled cups –
each blind within the fold of our defences,
numb, bristling, crushed in unstoppable freight,
careening off into ourselves, from which it's hard to return.

paired happiness – what a question,
what a change. allegedly what life is all about –
and yet the monster in me thought:
I can only tolerate t h i s m u c h closeness.
I don't want love like I say I do.

there's oneness and one ness –
whatever fear that keeps a soul from conjunction.
I'll tell you,
in the end it wasn't a relief – the feeling…
not depending on anyone else's choice of music.

left with all-night-spooky-thoughts of *out there*,
an eternal void links yesterday to tomorrow –
abysmal, 'til you slap on a filter, detach from truth, put on a show –
for emptiness is the sound of the world
when in the crowd you're on your own.

Confession

you know how you're supposed to 'know when you know?'
well, all I know about love is theoretical.
I'm practically certified, but knowing CPR
doesn't mean you'll save someone from drowning,
doesn't keep the water from *your* lungs,
so I'm faking it 'til I make it – getting off to 'documentaries'
human biology – just freakier.

I've been listening to a lot of rap lately
because boys keep breaking my heart – fuck them, right?
sometimes I think the love of my life is fame
and I've got chronic Other Woman syndrome
Powerful Woman syndrome –
I Don't Give A Shit About The Fact I'm Single syndrome.
all these ghosts are dead to me.

Phoebe Angeni

Up Late

I'm afraid or sad these nights,
thinking too much (again).
I find new ways to count the days
to occupy that construct – time,
as there's nothing to wake up for early.

I think a lot about my lungs,
the way my ribs expand,
enjoying the strength of them
to occupy that construct – time:
when there's nothing to wake up for early.

we find new ways to count the days
and meet here in A Moment,
where we all struggle to get by
(in one way or another)
remembering when we woke up early.

Shadows
7 haiku

Sidewalk at Sunset
asphalt and apricots –
fuzzy, blushed, and peeling
golden cracks in grey flesh

a snuffed red candle
slender fingers and smoke curls
like pale wedding rings

oh that midnight oil –
my head and hands together,
churning the moonlight

Darksong
primeval quiet –
a scream shaped space
emitting thick black air

the people I meet –
impressions of fingertips
on a cold window

Nothing!
I check my pages for words –
the whites of their eyes

Phoebe Angeni

When I Fucked-up the Cosmos

I don't know how, but I've shattered
the end off my pen,
which is a crying cosmic shame.

I need this colour: certainty
to sit by my bedside 'til morning

and watch me sleep. no one else is
breathing beside me,
besides my thirty year plan –

in the bin: splattered ink, cracked
innards, springs, plastic bits.

not exactly how I imagined it.
should I wake from this dream,
I won't transcribe it into sense –

distil nightmares to simple thoughts
pretty words, perfectly punctuated.

I won't have my pen. strange
how the vastness of the world calms me
down as much as it STRESSES ME OUT,

head up anxiety's ass, depending on *language* –
on *pens*, of all things.

Thoughts on Death

I laugh madness in the meantime,
brimming darktime,
when the bladder wakes you uptime
and it's tiptoe past the shutdoors time
because the lights are off but the dogs are on.

my first breath (unremembered)
Began somewhere beeping
and will Stop somewhere else.

tolling tolling Foretime
jolts electric - scythes the air
CLEAR as hospital machines
and whooping flocks of screambirds,
cackling crescents in the dark.

my first breath (unremembered)
was somewhere beeping
and somewhere else.

fridgetime bathes fluorescent yellow
on midnight angels' darker eyes
and holy mugs of something hot -
tongue burning Fivetime
Tolling madness in the dark.

As ever ceases, never starts
and only cycles with an N.

Slipping on Pearls

I wake and grieve the sun before it rises,
languish as I watch the cresting moon – suffering
to affix it to my memory.

I've mourned living love looking in their eyes
it's not seemly, I know – not what's done
but I do it.

not a nice thought but I have it –
like how I'm twined around the lattice of my mum:
without her

I'd simply go out – vanished – extinguished
a blip in the radar
once wound about grey hair, bitten nails, laugh lines

the faded pigment in her hands –
I need to remember them so I know we were here
to know that I exist – that this exists –

a pearl on the necklace of moments in time
double-wrapped around my wrists like shackles –
comfortingly linear, this moment, trapped here – alive.

Dead Plus One

I always say I'm one year older than I actually am.
maybe when I die I'll say I'm dead plus one.
that's a morbid thought,
but still funny –
don't worry – I'm not suicidal,

because none of us know where we go really
or what we'll do.
hell, maybe I'll die and do floral arrangements,
or become a stripper, or manage accounts,
or just sit brushing my teeth for eternity.

wouldn't that be a laugh:
all that hype and religion over minty fresh breath.
I wonder what kind of toothpaste dead dentists recommend?
It's 7:04am – what a strange way to start the morning –
maybe they use Oral-B.

Phoebe Angeni

An Echo

I woke up this morning missing you
went to sleep that way – if the two
of us were just not meant to be
why do I still love you (or think I do)
in my dreams, which are few, I see your face
that familiar ache
at arms length – loved
but not too close – pulling
strings for each other along
in one wrong way, or another

I woke up this morning hearing you
(although we don't speak)
the sound breaks what it finds in my mind
I blindly pick the wounds
to feel blood fresh upon my skin
something akin to love
on my tongue, which never tasted yours
to be yours –
we were so wrong
strung along through life by one another

Neither Here Nor There

I either pick at my nails or pick at my face
and call it curation –

an anxiety
for things that are there.

my brain often gets away
from my heart, or the facts –

which are empty
compared to things that aren't there.

I flipped through the pages I wrote
just to find you in them –

some semblance of your face
but you were never there.

people tell me it's a good thing –
that I should look ahead,

but any butterflies I had – I gave to you
or they're taxidermy. dead.

Spacelike

if my mind is an island, it's drifted
messily, independent of coordinates
depending on moments, meridians connecting them, the motion of the clock,
destined on the impossibility of a sunbeam

in an instant –
you have to be 100% honest with yourself.
I, for example, am writing this to stop washing away
second by second by sunrise, because the speed of light isn't fast enough

to join two disparate realities.
it was never my fault, or yours – deep down you know
we want the inaccessible, at least I do – did,
but now the physics of the world is different, and it should be

undoing old muscle memory, staring out at the dark
into spacelike skies, depending on moments –
meridians and motions of time so far unknown,
yet are fixed, are fate, are light.

Melancholy
5 haiku

capering quiet
laughing up my sleeves:
the cheek-pinching cold

finally outside,
kicking snow – the crocus bulb
in wellington boots

deep indigo night –
the moon's hooded face
holding a sickle

Elegy
ashes in a tin
siphoning ink from thin air,
making shapes from smoke

Night's dregs in a glass –
at the edge of her exhale
the blossoming sun

Phoebe Angeni

Before a Beginning

today I'm broken
but you already knew that
it could only be expected
now that you won't hold my hand

I clap politely for happy strangers

yesterday I ate a fishhook
because food tastes like shit
and I thought it, tugging in my guts,
would get me out of bed this morning

to clap politely for happy strangers

tomorrow's quiet space
on the park bench beside me
will play roulette with my memories
and all the while my vestigial heart

will beat politely for happy strangers

somehow, I loved you,
but I doubt you'd know that
I never thought I would have to let go
then again, now no one's holding my hand

I clap politely for happy strangers

Home from Work

ruddy dawn gently sways,
fading down the hall –
now twilight rose, she crumbles,
bleeding red into rain puddles,
reflective shallow swimming ice

fading down the hall –
now sunk to soul, steeped grey
as shadows grow monstrous.
she doesn't mind
the coat rack's friendly eyes.

now the cooling coals chuckle,
indulging love bites
and in the quiet night
birch bathes, bone-white –
fractured glass on faded cloth.

Phoebe Angeni

Upon reflection I do not miss you

In image, impression, hyper-fixation on ideals –
a ghost-like mirage, dangling
on the precipice of a petal-filled oasis.

I could still smell it if I wanted to –
like from the spray girls at Nordstrom
with the latest Yves St Laurent, ambrosial, synthetic, bottled.

I'm not shopping for that kind of perfume –
nostalgia-seeped, blowing through the busker's music, tingling amber-low afternoon
gaze, perching on pier's edge at low tide, daring, daunting, dissolving…

See, I can still go there if I want to.
I haven't wanted to for months –
things take the place of you –

Took the place
where I ripped you out, bare-handed grasping at the arteries, feeling each stretch and
snap as you pulsed away in my palm, thrown out over that very same pier – a calling?

an absence
an answer in itself – the most interesting part of a scene
I learned this with you – and how not everything means everything.

The Truth

is maybe I'm selfish, maybe we both were
seeing what we wanted,
avoiding reality for bluebells and whirling sand –
for a crystal carefully placed on my forehead,
longitude by latitude.

I think about it as I cross the sea
at the edge of the net, in the spider's web – tangents
from years away to minutes apart.
I won't ask you to meet me –
it's that loop I'm avoiding

where my brain won't allow me more than fantasy.
I had a talk with myself, you know – a nightmare
where I'm in your best man's chair (deluding myself)
in the *audience*, at the *back*, watching, loving you
pathetically, sadly, wrongly, stupidly
and I'll never tell you about it because that's the purpose of the talk.

you said I was too bright to reach.
I think some things are worth reaching for
if you really want them.
I think you didn't really want
me.

Phoebe Angeni

Only Cicadas, Water, and Salt

stars like the glow
of a thousand porch light-bulbs,
slightly grimy with dirt,
nothing expected – nothing to do
on either side of the shut screen door.

moths like turning pages
bashed against the window
towards daddy's beat-up lantern
still lit with promises
of early morning fishin.'

it's been a while since I properly cried,
untied – all edges and wrinkles,
a door to nowhere, opening –
the ceiling is low
but the light is natural.

At the Old House

Autumn began to look small in her bed and I knew
Winter would come – starting a cherry fire that blazed,
as he brushed his mittens clear of snow.

when the gnarled oak lost her leaves I knew
Winter was here – tucking the key under our mat,
as he shuffled his boots by the door.

I felt the chill of the meadow underfoot and I knew
the birds had gone and the wild geese were leaving,
so I ran to welcome him home.

About the Author

Phoebe Angeni is an emerging international poet and theatremaker.
Born in San Francisco, Angeni found her home in the East of
Scotland and now takes on projects in both America and the UK.
Angeni's work includes professional credits as a performer and
assistant director as well as the creator of a one-woman adaptation of
Homer's Odyssey, *Ithaca*, which premiered with five-star reviews at the
Edinburgh Fringe. Inspired by Classical and Pagan subjects as well as
avant-garde art movements such as Dadaism and Surrealism, Angeni's
poetry strives to break the literary fourth wall and create an intimate
relationship with its audience.

Phoebe Angeni holds a BA Honours in English Literature from the
University of St Andrews and has completed intensives at the Royal
Academy of Dramatic Art, London, and the Stella Adler Studio in
NYC. A (retired) certified yoga instructor and former barista, Angeni
can still craft a mean latte and design sweet vinyasa flows.

For more information and to get in touch please see:
www.phoebeangeni.com or @phoebe_angeni on all Social Media

Made in the USA
Las Vegas, NV
22 March 2023

69478379R00073